Other Books by Judy Juanita

The High Price of Freeways (short fiction)

Manhattan my ass, you're in Oakland (poems)

Virgin Soul (novel)

De Facto Feminism: Essays Straight Outta Oakland (essays)

Homage to the Black Arts Movement: a handbook

The African-American Experience in Four Genres: a handbook

Gawdzilla

Poems

Judy Juanita

EquiDistance Press
Oakland, CA

Gawdzilla
COPYRIGHT © 2022 Judy Juanita
EquiDistance Press, Oakland, CA

Book design:
Harper Design Group

Portrait photo on page 68:
Kingmond Young Photography

ISBN 978-1-7326098-0-8
Printed in the U.S.A.
November 2022

EquiDistance Press
490 Lake Park Ave.
P.O. Box 16053
Oakland, CA 94610
whoknewyouknew@gmail.com

Dedicated to my mentors in
The Bergen Poets in New Jersey
I offer gratitude for healing from
my poet-mentors who are gone:

Dorothy Good, John Calabrese, Lois Van Houten,
Juanita Tobin, Steve Komeshek, Ruth Falk,
Alice Kolb, Max Greenberg, Mike Reardon,
Laura Boss, and Stephen Dunn.

You gave the precious gifts of friendship,
camaraderie and tender guidance.
I came in that Thursday night,
April 24, 1980, battered by life's storms.
It took a few years and more than a
few powwows at assorted Jersey diners,
but I walked away restored.

Table of contents

Preface

I've been a member of the Soka Gakkai International-USA for over 40 years and believe fervently in the sanctity of life. Some time after my youthful and equally fervent participation in the Black Panther Party, I became a Nichiren Soka Gakkai Buddhist. SGI Second President Josei Toda's call for "death" to those who would use nuclear weapons can be misconstrued if the context isn't given. I include the context from the website, https://www.joseitoda. org/vision/declaration/background.html, as a preface to *Gawdzilla* which equates the film monster Godzilla metaphorically with the evils of imperialism.

"Although a movement calling for a ban on the testing of atomic or nuclear weapons has arisen around the world ... I want to expose and rip out the claws that lie hidden in the very depths of such weapons. I wish to declare that anyone who ventures to use nuclear weapons, irrespective of their nationality or whether their country is victorious or defeated, should be sentenced to death without exception. Why do I say this? Because we, the citizens of the world, have an inviolable right to live. Anyone who jeopardizes that right is a devil incarnate, a fiend, a monster." – *Josei Toda in a speech calling for the abolition of nuclear weapons in 1957 in Yokohama, Japan.*

He encouraged the 50,000 youth present that day to do their best to spread the anti-nuclear spirit throughout the world.

The website comments: "Toda denounced those who would use nuclear weapons as 'devils' in the Buddhist sense of 'robbers of life' and nuclear weapons themselves as the embodiment of absolute evil. His stance was that nuclear weapons and their use must be absolutely condemned, not from the standpoint of ideology, nationality or ethnic identity but from the universal dimension of humanity and our inalienable right to live."

The website also cites the military journalist and critic Tetsuo Maeda: "Inside second Soka Gakkai President Toda's heart, the authoritarian power of the militarist clique before the war and the power of the superpowers' nuclear arsenals overlapped with each other. He must have seen the nuclear weapon as the same unreasonable, devilish authority as the military clique that had trampled the desire for peace and freedom of religion, and brought oppression and hardship in prison upon Toda himself. This therefore led to his straightforward confrontation against 'absolute evil' and the fundamentally uncompromising battle against those who threaten people's right to live. And here lies the discernment of a man of religion for a new era."

Gawdzilla

godzilla

*American nuclear weapons testing has
created a seemingly unstoppable,
dinosaur- like beast* **Godzilla, 1954**

on rainy Saturdays
we watched one godzilla movie
after another

while mommy and daddy
fought the race battle
with every ounce of their marriage

daddy was fired for speaking out
mommy rubbished for working
her fingers to the bone

we only wanted her lemon
meringue pie on Sunday
and rainy Saturday godzilla

by the end of the movie
godzilla would die in a prolonged fit
splashing his finicles

screaming at the clock tower
the wharf
the san francisco bay

her wrist had a cyst
daddy's was at his temple
your mummy hit me with a frying pan

ha-ha
the sun would come back out
we'd run back out to hopscotch

play hide-and-go-seek
until the clouds burst again
and tv beckoned us back

godzilla rose like gorilla jesus
even though G-men with machine guns
had shot him dead (they did, didn't they?)

mommy and daddy's racism
remained, sturdy as Godzilla
who died a loud screeching death

when the Oxygen Destroyer
liquefied his bones before
we ate chili mac and crackers

all the while mommy and daddy double-dosed
implacable racism with brown v. bd of ed
topeka, ks, and impeccable good manners

     you so ugly yo mama named you godzilla

return of godzilla

The monsters make their way towards Osaka
as Japan can only brace for tragedy and
relive the horror of Godzilla once more
Godzilla Raids Again, 1955

when we thought it had sunk to the bottom
of the deep blue sea godzilla reared
that ugly head and shocked the shit out of us
we watched the black and white movie pop-eyed
as black people were hoisted by hoses in Mississippi
m-I-S-S-I-S-S-I peepee in your eye
unfaltering racism/uglier than godzilla's scales

yo house so ugly godzilla don't want it for free

godzilla forgotten

A UN reporter broadcasts a report on the appearance
of a prehistoric monster that emerges from hibernation
while a pharmaceutical company seeks
publicity with a monster of their own.
King Kong vs. Godzilla, 1963

we forgot tv during the sixties
our lives were live-action movies
dancing in the streets
molotov cocktails in the streets
partying in the streets
hollering at the govt in the streets
making love everywhere

what do that damn godzilla wont? the world for starters

godzilla adapts

A reporter on a tropical island discovers an infant monster
that Godzilla must adopt and learn to raise as one of his own
Son of Godzilla, 1967

we made a revolution and lost our ever loving minds
the viet nam soldiers came home in pine boxes
we raged against the machine fought the power

it felt like losing a leg

we learned anew to
rise
stand
walk
kneel
eat
heal
hum
fight
cool it down
bounce back
from tragedy

I know demons

*A submarine expedition to salvage the remains of Mechagodzilla
is thwarted by a massive dinosaur named Titanosaurus.*
Terror of Mechagodzilla, 1975

I know demons
I know dem
I know him

he don't look like Godzilla
he look like God
he bring me bounty
in a beautiful body
not scaled and hard
soft and deep brown
handsome curved slender
hip bone sheathed in silky
skin above the iliac crest

he makes beautiful love
he comes after I come
waiting patiently
his gift thrusting softly
I go out of my mind when
he is inside me
pumping sucking pushing
thrusting on the downstroke

handsome man and I fight the devil
the white man together
all demons exist outside our oneness

but demons go everywhere
I try on a wig to see what it feels like

I hate it he insists I wear it
during sex he snatches it off
laughing like a demon

sex becomes a chore unless
I imagine other men in me
our arguing sets fires inside the oneness
our revolutionary fervor turns
to rage against each other
sex becomes torture
I turn out to be demon's other half

he slaps me/hard
I have no one to tell
I wake-up with him inside me
pushing my face to the side
this beloved knocks me
to the floor when I refuse sex
refuse to fix dinner
keep the bathroom door closed
demons push open all doors
claim ownership
dominion

I know demons
I know dem
I know him

    When I get my mind back, I leave Godzilla

ours

Thirty years after the original monster's rampage,
a new Godzilla emerges and attacks Japan
Godzilla 1985

ours was the next-to-worst house on the block...my parents college-educated
...dad a compulsive gambler... money came in, mom a hardworking civil
servant...it went back out...he pawned the tv, irons, radios, mother's sewing
machines, brother's suits, bicycles, you name it... four kids...it was a struggle...before we got part time jobs...when Richie Valens and the Big Bopper
died in a plane crash...I came home with my best friend to watch American
Bandstand...dad had carted the tv off to the pawn shop...I was ashamed...
he used to pack Spam on pancakes for our lunch pails...I was ashamed...
both were readers...the public library another home...books were always in
abundance...but it was agonizing to be these bright overachieving kids...
come home to lights turned off...phone cut off...creditors hounding my
mother...garbage collection cut off...we hauled our own garbage with dad
to the city dump...I moved as far away as I could before I could fathom that
they adored us...made sure we got good educations...always had that house
to come home to...I never lose the habit of shopping at thrift stores...where
every so often my eye falls on a godzilla toy...

who fuck Godzilla unless they super horny?

12

a prayer to Godzilla

godzilla of the urban nightmare
godzilla of outsized space
give us this dream our daily dream
give us the dream of being
(the dream of supervision atop the dream of being)
nowIlaymedowntosleepIpraythelordmysoultokeep
We're trying to pray
oh my god / god my oh
god awful thoughts stagger (through) us
      gawd is a big fat showoff
      gawd is always late for work
      can we fire gawd for absenteeism?
oh my gawd is that blasphemy?

it's spelled differently
oh my god no no no no
andifidiebeforeiwakeipraythelordmysoultotake
gawdzilla doesn't have ears
is that on purpose?

gawdzilla likes catastrophe
cruel jokes
destruction
death and all the angels of death

cities on fire
scaring people to death
being a laughable hero
being mistaken for a hero
is that on purpose?

being a hero
calling himself hero of the world
going around the world

beating his chest
toppling buildings and govts.
being benevolent after the fact

my gawd, he is full of himself
is that on purpose?

the powerful nurse, the powerful baby

da baby talks in the hospital drainage
I coulda been a contender
a half-baby quarter-baby
eighth-baby sixteenth-baby
da baby sticks around
waiting for the nurse to come back
he remembers her orange dansko clogs

she can talk to the world
about how he drowned
da baby waits for her to come back
but she works four days on three days off
he's jealous of whole babies
screaming in expectation
on the other floor
he wants to join their club
       nobody wants you not even gawdzilla
da baby has to join his kind
in the sewage pipes of los angeles nyc chicago
in the pipes 22 inches below the top ground
da baby would settle to be an atonement baby
an after three miscarriages baby
da baby wanted wholeness
he wouldn't have minded being
ugly as gawdzilla
to be alive
to eat mush and grow teeth
to gather fuzz between his toes
instead of guts swirling around him

when the shift changes
da baby becomes a rush of dirty water
the drainage clears the dream of being
once and again

how did I get pregnant haiku

all my babies
were rhythm
babies

oompy doompy who you be

when i sing my oompy doompy song
am i just nina simone off key?
aretha with a properly fitted bra?

if i pop my pistol
oompy doompy one two three
will a flag bullet come out?

can i be fannie lou hamer
without the trail of the deep
south behind me?

can i get the ghost of
ntozake shange
without the anguish?

who I be if I be anybody at all?
nobody? who dat? oompy
doompy making peace/with my self

old black woman

she got a kick out of godzilla
but her favorite show was lassie
said white people love their dogs so much
because it was bred in them
to treat blacks like beasts
of burden during slavery
come reconstruction they tried
but couldn't adapt
postbellum and jim crow
they tried but needed pets
to quiet the beast within
she noticed that when lassie died
his replacements looked exactly
the same
but godzillas
look different each time

en pleine air

in 2019 merchants in
kansas traded memorabilia:
$324,500 for a quarter-plate daguerreotype
of enslaved people carting cotton
in woven wicker baskets

before we were memorabilia
skulls lips noses genitalia
en pleine air
we were perpetual mourners
grotesqueries
raw footage for the amerikkkan dream
displayed like godzillas
our scars filling daguerreotypes
as cannibals tore crisply blackened
skin from the sweet magnolia tree of life

ah! bourgeois shopkeepers photo'd in daylight
nooses tightened necks snapped posing
deathly polite en pleine air for postcards
like post-production still photography

the postal service wouldn't ban lynching cards until 1908
the business of slavery being business
　　　　brisk then brisk now
as daughters of the amerikkkan revolution erected
high monuments to remind *the nigras* of their proper place and posture

what him last name?

franklin
washington
lincoln
lincoln
lincoln
lincoln
lincoln
jackson
        the dream of being
taylor
mckinley
hamilton
adams
harrison
        until slavery ended
        many didn't have a last name
        afterwards nobody name a baby
benjamin godzilla or george godzilla or abraham godzilla
        that wouldn't be nice

prolly

prolly been on the streets since she fostered out
at twelve
12 not 18
she been a ho
prostitute strawberry
slut hooker tramp hussy
never had intercourse
she gives head
like a specialty
her front teeth knocked out
cops don't give a fuck
they only want her gums
nicknamed her pro'ly
her answer to any questions
probably
shortened to pro'ly
then prolly
one trick got so enraged
he knocked her in the mouth
sent pieces of tooth all over
her down her
throat
        bitch, don't you know how to talk?
kept hitting until
her teeth looked like
a crocodile's mouth
she stayed at a shelter
where a counselor told her
she chose to come back in this life
as a particular kind of woman

and know how it feels to suffer
prolly didn't understand
but appreciated the extra vouchers
the nice lady gave her

counselor

prolly's counselor has grey sprouts in her hair
means no harm
makes what some call excuses
      I don't know   maybe so   life is...
      pivoting doesn't mean you don't have a plan
her definitive protest statement
      I live my life at flea markets
her secondhand boots kick ass
her protests are her umpteen pairs of boots
her obitchuary will list them by color
friends will be encouraged to pick a pair as souvenir

oasis

people know better
but plead ignorance
I'm talking san francisco
where tourists with icons of the golden gate
in their heads, arrive to streets cleansed
with urine and wine
whose biggest shock is not the homeless
papering the streets
but their own sleeveless naïveté
and the wind
these ruthless consumers shiver
on double decker tourist buses
ignoring toothless urban troops
woman in gutter with bloated stomach
scruffy agrarian in beat up van
ubers drop off the flush big tippers
in polo ralph lauren and seersucker pants
pursuing faux farmers with organic peaches
showering for dinners they will brag about
when they leave the nightmare
and the godzilla-mind recalls the dream

why my son's babymama won't read my books

mom, her book club reads man-hating
preacher-cheating-on-their-wives
cheesy-romance
ghetto-erotica

godzilla love him some publishing

godzilla births female orangutans

a kardashian butchers her face into
a kewpie doll with our lips
another apes us with silicone butt

mocking us and the slavemasters who auctioned us naked
inserting the middle finger to show our fertility

one nestles a brown baby against that recast jaw
triggering envy hate monstrous anger
our reproach: you hold our brown baby too much
she is defiant: *we good*

nah
you good
we not

the biggest difference is not the money

*(on seeing robert palmer's hands clutching
a cigarette two days before he died)*

the biggest difference is not
the best selling records
the chart-topping sales
the stadium tours
the vacuous interviews like they're geniuses
not hustlers or products of hustlers
changing *I Shot the Sheriff*
from protest freedom anthem
to celebration of guitar virtuosity
the biggest difference is not the pure
capitalism of elvis and his forbidden sex
versus the wide open sex of big mama thornton
the biggest difference is not retiring
in midlife in palm springs and jersey
versus working the casinos until they drop dead at 77

the biggest difference is the unknuckled
uncalloused soft white hands

swimming towards godzilla, swimming from godzilla

the legs are the second heart / robust young males swim to safety
in the great Mediterranean / they dog paddle to freedom
      the women and babies scream and sink
      into eternity / a few feet from the raft
young black men in classrooms / use their hamstrings and deltoids
to cross the great Oakland LA / Kentucky ocean to become the next
Odell Beckham Stefon Diggs / cannon fodder for capitalists

huddling young fellas yelp and dive from the midnight ferries
to reach Greece / kicking splashing to master the promise
the ones in Oakland frown and squat pull up curse while
girlfriends and babies hold on for dear life in Deep East

a motorized rubber raft leaves Libya on Wednesday
land is heaven   water is hell
the raft collapses on Thursday
74 disappear / two ballers make division one

the blesséd curséd float
momentarily
before tasting brine in the deep oceanic

to meet godzilla

daniela stands before the class to answer their prepared questions:
    what were you thinking when you were robbing the bank?
    what did the note say – "I want all the money"?
    didn't you have family or relatives that could've loaned you the
    money?
    how did you get the courage to go through with the robbery?
    were drugs involved in your decision to do it?
    when you served your sentence, how did you feel?
    was it worth the money?
    did you regret it?
    after all this, where is your thought on law school?
    do you think it was destiny for you to go and steal money in order to
    help others once time had passed?
    what did you do that made you start getting bad grades?
    why rob a bank? why not, for example, prostitute?
    did you think you would be successful?
    was prison easy or hard? were you uncomfortable?
    how much time did you serve? did you get paroled?

in her own defense

dancing folklorico
working at costco
volunteering
striving for law school
doing too much
        I started failing
        lost my financial aid
        I felt like I was failing everyone
        I saw a robbery on *law & order*
        went to the bank with a note
        it happened like I was in a movie
        the bank teller handed me thousands of dollars
        I paid bills
        I did it one more time
        then I got caught
when she leaves the students swear
she did it more than twice
she comes back several semesters
less open each time
until she moves away

lizzo fights godzilla

we is 100% behind you baby girl
behind your superb black ass
behind your exponential black ass
behind all the big black women
we who are beybey
we who are beybey's kids
we who raised beybey
who raised beybey's babies and babydaddies
we behind you lizzo

show that ass
put that ass on the lakers scoreboard
for the world to see
your big fat cocoa ass
as important for the world to see as
emmett till's bludgeoned face
"let them see what they did to my boy
let the world see what they did to my boy"

let us worship lizzo
that's right — bow down
before her big black ass
before her big black booty
not injected into her backside by a dominican doctor
not leaking formaldehyde into her veins clotting her heart
killing one more big fat implacable life
fuck brazilian butt lifts
fuck the strip clubs that hire the women
who pay with their very life for butts
that sit high on their hips
21st century venus hottentots
fuck the only way these women will earn $2,000 a night $3,000 a night $4,000
a night

instead of working at walmart
(yeah yeah yeah do the math $15@ hr. times 30 hrs a week so they don't have
to give them health benefits. that's $450 a week, $1800 a month, the living
wage that biden is fighting for? get real. you'd hop on a plane to the dominican republic, leak silicone all over the seats armrests tray tables too for a big
black ass a big black ass)
    lizzo's black ass is worth gold
    diamonds and gucci
    in the belly of the beast
    same place where
    lizzo's army yeah
    a black only army for the descendants of buffalo soldiers and tuske-
    gee airmen
    a big black beautiful army whose big black unbleached asshole
    emits the noxious gases called life, liberty and the pursuit of
    happiness.
    same place where corner stores have filled those asses for decades
    with hostess twinkies butterfingers koolaid fruit loops sodas hogmaw
    and chitlins hot links potato salad macaroni and cheese sweet potato
    pie...beybey's son the athlete/personal trainer says with disgust, ma,
    this is carbo overload, but eats at the christmas table because he too
    worships lizzo once a year

    we love you lizzo
    our anti-lady godiva
    our anti-kardashian
    our anti-american

    miss america?
    you the missing america
    the antidote to self-loathing
    you had to be huge
    in our face

all over the place
you are the dream deferred no more
you cannot be invisible
you will not live underground
not one more day

lizzo our lizzo
lizzo lizzo lizzo lizzo lizzo
you is you is you is
amerikkka the beautiful.

godzilla 2022

just because woolworth's lunch counters were
integrated and black people could buy lunch there
didn't mean that woolworth's wasn't fading

just because blacks integrated the academy awards
and slapped each other silly doesn't
mean the institution of hollywood isn't fading

kevin costner preaches to the minions with gravitas
and brags about being 68 during the awards while
the sell by date for females in hollywood is 38 or so

the real problem is that hollywood is
as out-of-date
an institution as slavery.
but because it's so profitable
for the slave-owners
it hasn't faded out completely

but its time is up

godzilla as destiny

billionaires millionaires the amerikkkan dream
up, up and away onto the edge of space
horatio alger wins again
rags-to-riches
poor boy sandwiches
raggedy ann dolls
immigrants in shacks
children in cages
we love it all, eh?
up, up and away
the bigger the better
the farther from the crime scene
the better. and the edge of space is
the mall of america.
opportunity our national anthem
except except tulsa in 1920-when? 1921
black people black dynasties
black millionaires buying and flying
their own airplanes
black businesses black prosperity
and we prostrate ourselves

for a black face on the $20 bill
eh?
ask the black okies
about the grand downtown they built
especially for the bombs
dropped especially on tulsa

listen to the sound of bombs
bursting in air
ask the black oakies
then forward to philly in 1990-what?

1990-when? 1990-why?
when a black mayor dropped bombs
on wild haired ramona africa
an american millionaire, no?
rags to riches, no?
horatio alger, no?
MOVE the antithesis of progress
cleanliness
we, the deodorant-rich country
watching televised spectacles
little blue-and-white suited people
blast past the boundary of space
the richest man in the world
thanks his wage slaves and customers
for paying for it all

and all is forgiven because why?
because
when the land ran into the pacific ocean
manifest destiny shot into space

found poem from daughter of ntozake shange

My mother struggled with staying alive, and each day was a kind of win.
Even if she wasn't ever truly happy, she taught me to touch joy. Even if she
never really was okay, she taught me that it was worth sticking it out all the
same....She died after traveling for work for ten out of the last fifteen days of
her life — at seventy years old. At her last gig, she told me she felt abused —
not because anyone was unkind or rude — but because of the brutal schedule.
This world just kept taking from her, as she traipsed through a conference
hotel with a walker and a wheelchair and congestive heart failure and a
haunted nervous system because there were still poems that needed to be
read and rent that needed to be paid. She deserved better than the extractive
economy of being a surviving artist, better than a dystopian celebrity culture
that doesn't know how to care for a manic-depressive, self-medicating Black
prophetess. We all do.
She was ecstatic when I signed the contract for Progressive Dystopia...

Savannah Shange in *Progressive Dystopia:*
Abolition, Antiblackness, and Schooling in San Francisco

Ann the truthteller

just cuz I'm out here
on the street
you think I'm pitiful
a diseased scaly monster
I could have a million dollars
in a mattress
        if I had a mattress
Ann not begging
Ann talking
all the philosophers not in the ivory tower
just like not all christians in church

Ann naming babies

Max. That's what I like about white people. They keep the same name generation after generation, Max, Max, Max, Max, Henry the first, Henry the second, Henry the eighth. They names is not confusing. They don't care if the little baby look up at em all funny, like Mabel? Why you giving me this tired name again? We do different. We go whichever way we get enslaved. *Wha massa name? John? Das my name.* We get with the French and we name ourselves Denise, Charmaine, Elouise. We get with the Irish and it's Siobhan, Mickey. We went Swahili, evbody had Cumbuka, emboli-all them names sound like they got booger or booty up in em. Haki Madhubootie. So now we got all these twenty somethings running around with Ay-rab names. Ahmed, Muhammad, Siddiqi. They just sounded different before Sept. 11: Khalid, Abdul, and Hasan. Now it sounds like your grandson is on the 22 Most Wanted List. And if you go to the Post Office and look at the faces, you don't see Amad al-sheik Abdullah. You see Miz Jones' nephew what been living with her since he got out of prison. Or Tommy Green who six feet eight and cain't play basketball. And white folks still naming babies Thomas and Jefferson and George. And here Ann test. The Mexicans never enslaved us but show me a black baby name José.

Ann and Emmett Till

I grew up on Emmett Till and JET magazine
Since when did folks get so fucking innocent
they can't see blood and suffering?
JET was the only place that would publish
the burnt up corpses of the lynched Negroes
the only place where you could see Emmett Till body
all laid up in the funeral home
where his mama said
Let the whole world see what they done to my boy
As I recall, some folk used to hold lynch parties
make picture postcards out of the poor burnt up bodies.
some folks mean as snakes

Ann and the Namibians

You can be picky when you got it good. I had it good. Ann didn't always be out here like a wild dog. I had a house and a family. My luck got bad and then it disappeared. Nobody wants ya when ya down and out. You need to meet the Namibis...I saw these Namibi refugees on TV. Black as midnight. So black they were blue. Beautiful. Stunning Black. And a white lady from Paly Alto was showing them around a park, a nice, big walking and jogging park down there near Stanford. And she was just a showing them how to go walking in this trail that was all winding and getting into darkness. And one of them Namibis said, "Will I get eaten if I go in there?" Ain't that nice? Afraid of lions and tigers. We not afraida lions and tigers. We got bigger problems. Wait till he gets pestered to death walking past the homeless. Funk. Dirt. We more scared of dirt than lions and tigers. We got guns and zoos. We tame wild animals. I got things worse than funk. But if you never get to know me, you'll never find em.

Ann on unemployment

Negroes don't wont jobs, they don't wont full employment. Unemployment is self-medication for Negroes. We get fired, "Fuck it. I didn't want this job no way." We would go stark raving mad if all us had to work every day. That demands yo attention. And Negroes don't wanna pay attention cuz when they do they damn near trampled into extinction. We better off unemployed. And Ann a prime example. Ann not drowning in credit-card debt. Ann don't have no phone to get turned off. Ann mortgage not worrying her to death. And Ann not getting high blood from trying to keep up with the Joneses. And Ann ain't had a job since Hector was a pup.

Ann goes to church

a white woman I know, one a my buddies...she big, got dishwater hair. On
Sunday, she go up and down where the black churches are. First she go
inside the open front door and estimate where in the service the pastor is. She
know bout call and response. She know where the climax. Then she walks
out wif her cane and her waddle. She bold. She go round the back door and
check to see if it's a feast waiting for the Sunday go-to-meeting folk. Cuz she
know bout black churches. *A-maz*, white folk church over, *Zing*, White folk
be out the door, *Grace*, white folk be at the Sizzler eating dinner, *How Sweet*,
it Monday morn, white folk at work, *The sound*, white folk be done got they
paycheck and black folk still in church. And she help herself and keep on
down the street, as resolute as a street dog. She been doing this for years, say
her only good meal is on Sunday morning in the black community.

godzilla of innocence

How did white Americans get to be so innocent? *Why do they hate us? Why would they kill innocent people?* A while back a white woman went to get her prescription filled in the middle of the night in Oakland on Telegraph Ave. Now that's bad enough right there. As a black person I would be watching my back just on account of that. But this woman-God rest her innocent pure soul-takes her recycling to the back of the Walgreen's at midnight after getting her prescription filled. I know she must have been in pain to be out at that time of night but as luck would have it a crackhead comes up and blows her away. Very sad, but again I ask, when did white folks get so fucking innocent? With the blood of four centuries of oppression and war and what do you call that when you take somebody's land and call it your own –appropriation? And I know white folks love to say, *but I never owned slaves I never did that That was over 150 years ago*…I grew up in East Oakland I was never a slave I never picked cotton or got paid in chittlins and hog maw but I know from whence I came and the road that led here…And here we go again with this guy in the CIA, this innocence this fucking innocence. Why? Johnny Mike Spann. He was 29 years old. Wanted to be in the CIA or FBI since high school. Where did he get this notion? Only two of two places: movies and tv. He was watching reruns of "The Man from U.N.C.L.E." and "The Saint" with Roger Moore, not to mention Tarzan, the original CIA, the template for the CIA, Bwana. This was the pattern in his little blond head. That's why two CIA, with their pistol-blond Johnny is so proud to be one of them-step up in front of a crowd of captured Taliban with a simple-assed question, Why are you here? A real John Wayne moment on non-John Wayne turf. Of course all hell breaks loose and while Spann kills three of them, they stomp and bite, yes, bite, yes, bite him to death. "Mission Impossible" never ended like that. "Secret Agent" man? It's very powerful when our fantasies come true. It's very dangerous when our fantasies come true because it's very unreal when our fantasies come true.

brown people white people black people red people yellow people

what are these crayola colors we've accepted
as if people were actually tomato-red
or yolk-yellow?

Why can't we (all just get along?) fall into
a beautiful decorator's palette
...oh my fawking gawdzilla!
Are we nothing more
than backup singers for buttercups
chrysanthemums and those egotistical
eggplants?

Is it a stroke of imagination to call
flesh-and-blood (flesh-colored Band-Aid wearing) people
red and yellow?
although I have seen
some sheet-white Caucasians
who seem a shock even to themselves
but if we want to go there
let's create new people in all the
Benjamin Moore colors:

"I have a friend in Seattle, a mauve.
She's so into rain she glistens in the mist.
But I, a charcoal, look like a wet ashtray
when I visit her."

"I'm crazy about the new guy. What a pumpkin."
"Are you sure he's not a yam? Or even a sweet potato?"
"He's the offspring of a puce and an evergreen."
"My parents are a magenta and a bamboo."
"I heard both families objected to that union."
"But love won out and then came me

the lilac, my sister, a poppy seed
and baby brother
our antelope."

d.j. raw product

Yeah, went to get a burrito in Berkeley and next door the white boys were playing John Coltrane, no, a John Coltrane score. Hah! Sheet music. Shit Music!! If I never took a lesson held a clarinet tuba snared a drum bruised a thumb playing on a trumpet trying to be Dizzy Gillespie I gotta watch? Watch, ma' fucker, no I ain't gotta watch nothing. I'm a player. I ain't dead. I know niggas was fabulous raw product for the last 400 years and capitalism functions high white and mighty off raw product. Capitalism say, we got to commodify John Coltrane. Put his shit down on paper, sell it, buy it, store it, CD it, stream it, and then we don't need John. Die, mafucker, for all we care. We will build you an edifice called smooth jazz and on your tombstone put: NIGGERS WATCHED SLAVED AND FORGOT THEY DREAMS. Go eat a burrito, mafucker, with hi tech no sauce, we can't be commodified because we free even if some of us gotta die to get that freedom.

Barney, the gawdzilla-training toy

I take little Jo-Jo to see a real live Barney. All the kiddies are so excited. They have their little purple Barneys, singing that goofy song, all their mothers, aunties, grandmas-one or two daddies-all ready to see Barney. This great six foot five Barney, looking like a dinosaur with purple carpeting, comes out and all the kids start bawling. Boo-hooing. Shivering. Scared shitless. Jo-Jo jumps on my chest, his little heart thumping away. Terrified. One thing to see Barney on the TV set every day at daycare. A horse of a different color to see this great big old purple people-eating megasaurus. They never do get those kids quieted down. The closer he comes to them, they more they freak out-gawdzilla, in small measure, confronted directly by children. The terrible irony is that the adults, we who've fought gawdzilla all our damn lives, howl. Bowled over, pitifully cracking up. Hysterical with laughter. I haven't laughed that hard in a month of Sundays. It brings tears to my eyes.

coping with gawdzilla haiku

I've been dopey
off love dopey off drugs
give me love

dave chappelle

you're looking
malcolmish
dave

if only you hadn't walked
from fifty million dollars
empire wouldn't have known

if only you'd been ridiculous
you could be feted
and ignored by all

if malcolm had been mediocre
not stood up to empire
he would be almost 100 years old

while you buck empire over and over
making your black ass
a target

empire smiles all malcolmish
giving any judas permission to kill
ask malcolm

standing in the audubon ballroom
looking malcolmish
knowing what was coming

I try not to keep seeing jesus

I try not to keep seeing jesus
on the mean streets of san fran
seeing him there makes me hate gutters
why isn't he black like the wooly haired jesus in the black churches?
I keep seeing him white as old caked dirt
I could bathe his nasty self
make him white as snow
But he's too mean to touch let alone scrub
I keep seeing him (dat not babyjesus)
I keep seeing this snarly man
evil as a woman who just found
her man in bed with another man
(him so evil his mama don't want him)
and he curses his father
every time he looks to the heavens
sends a tail of comets
up gawd's ass out of pure spite

give him a plain name like rahim
who cares if it's muslim?
and, my gawd, decapitalize it

when godzilla booted nixon out of the oval office

lawyers and secretaries stood at the juncture
caught in the frisson of empire changing hands
young jewish lawyers earnest about civil liberties
      poor for a minute and horny/suspended
      in space between law school and their life-to-be
sharply dressed black secretaries
      privy to everyone's secrets/which is to say
      completely powerless/unless inclined
      to blow jobs and quickies at the juncture
it looked like a permanent mosaic
complete with the local black militant
in his socialist phase who marches/into the office for cash
like it was guerilla warfare/sweeps past the secretaries
(soon to be replaced by computers)
secretaries tasked to visit the biggest donor's big mansion
he writes the biggest check, asks if they want ice cream
in the blink of an eye rings a bell
a colored maid in uniform
comes down and serves them
her hair askance
top button unbuttoned
eyeballs rolling
at the two black women
she serves
before she leaves
in a huff
and the talking goes on

arming for armageddon and godzilla

I put everything she taught me in a snow globe
and turn it upside down
       never let a man use you for a pisspot
       I brush my nipples against men's chests
your lips are too big for red lipstick
never wear red, you're too dark
       I look at red dresses forever
       buy one and wear it for years
do you know how ugly you really are?
and white people don't have flat feet
       a white girl blond and giggly
       orders spumoni in front of me standing
       on white feet flatter than pancakes
years later I read how in slavery the mothers protected
their young daughters from rape by the slavemaster:
you is ugly, never forget how ugly you is

haiku after gawdzilla

heaven is after
all is said and done
a tiny place

gawdzilla's integration haiku

assimilation
degradation
bitches & hoes

Obitchuary: James Ambrose Johnson Jr.

Rick James *Super Freak* died Aug. 6, 2004. "Toxicology and the presence of the following drugs: (Xanax), (Valium), (Wellbutrin), (Vicodin), Digoxin, methamphetamine and cocaine...None of the drugs or drug combinations were found to be at levels that were life threatening in and of themselves. The cause of death was ruled acute cardiac dysfunction due to an enlarged heart. The coroner said he didn't die of a drug overdose."

The Gun as Ultimate Performance Poem

George Zimmerman killed Trayvon Martin, was acquitted for it, and has now switched from security guard to painter, boxer, butcher, baker, candle-stick-maker, whatever he wants. One round point blank to the chest = a perfect exchange. A young life for his art. The Gun as art and culture.

The Gun as work of art. The Gun as art form and genre. The Gun makes history. The Gun as steel metaphor carrying the human urge to dominate and lay waste to an enemy or perceived threat. Guns as import and export. Hollywood's Gun, its cinematic ordnance, is the United States' international calling card.

The Gun is oh-so-social as it erases human inequality. Anyone can obtain one and point...shoot...kill. A bullet has no name, face, race, gender or class. The Gun is its microphone, the shooter but the stand for the microphone. The bullet is absolute, life-ending or life-changing, irreversible. The Gun is clean, leaving only smoke and powder in its wake. The Gun is the ultimate perfor-mance poem; the message in the poem is the bullet.

As much as I think I'm peaceable, I keep falling in with The Gun.

I moved back to my parents' house in East Oakland in 1990, in the middle of an intense drug war. My childhood home was a stone's throw from the notorious projects where heroin kingpin Felix Mitchell, as head of the 69 Mob, created an industry of drug trafficking as efficient for a decade as Henry Ford's assembly line. Felix the Cat's death in 1986 had left a fierce turf war in its wake. The nightly sequence I heard from my writing desk was spine-chilling: rapid machine gun fire, a car burning rubber as it screeched into the dark, silence for 10-12 minutes, then the ambulance siren. I never heard screams. Why were there no screams?

Without the noble purpose I conceived guns to have when I was a young black militant, without art or revolutionary credo, these were unbearable microphones for a shattering community. Guns. Guns. Guns. I had liked guns.

Decades earlier, while a college junior, I joined the Black Panther Party in 1967 right when it split from a rival group of black cultural nationalists. Malcolm X's widow, Betty Shabazz, had come to San Francisco that February for a celebration of his life. One group called itself the Black Panther Party of Northern California, the other the Black Panther Party for Self-Defense; each agreed to meet her plane at the San Francisco airport with guns to protect her. One group showed up with loaded guns, the second came unloaded. The second group had no art, no ability to make history, no message. Though the second group was full of poets, writers, intellectuals and bright young minds, the first group prevailed, and Huey Newton, Bobby Seale and Eldridge Cleaver joined the pantheon of holders of The Gun. The activists upstaged the artists/intellectuals. I had immense sympathy for the second group, but pitied them (Pitied their women more. How much subservience would soothe a wounded ego?). The Gun was the shatterer of the boundary between the personal and the political. I liked guns. They were talismanic and palm-friendly. I liked being clandestine, carrying that .22 in my clutch purse when I went to work at the post office. The BPP labeled the intellectuals "paper panthers." This conflict between conscience and activism is not new. Stephen Spender, writing about the Oxford intellectuals said "detached intelligence" was a stance that a generation of anti-Fascists in the 1920s and 1930s rejected. "Personal values had to be sacrificed to the public cause. All that mattered was to defeat Fascism….choices had to be decided by the Marxist interpretation of history. Subjective motives did not count."

The split between the two groups of black militants shattered the viability of "detached intelligence" in the San Francisco Bay Area. The BPP cut through the pacifistic and rhetorical gestures and stance of the cultural nationalists with the pragmatism of the bullet. It resolved the issue of activism. How active should an activist be? Ready to die for the cause. The BPP resurrected the spirit of Nat Turner, Sojourner Truth and Harriet Tubman. The latter told her charges who wanted to return to the plantation once they'd gone underground: If you turn back, I'll shoot you.

The idea of carrying a loaded gun in May 1967 into the legislative chambers of Sacramento, the dominion of Governor Ronald Reagan, into the harsh deadly face of mid 20th century racist stolidity, rocked the world. Thirty black men, armed to the teeth and dressed in the signature beret and leather jackets, had the kind of impact that suicide bombers or serial killers have today. Scary.

The Gun is a revolt of the mind, an expulsion of hatred and thus a cleansing agent. Once it is fired, the act done, the two opposites are united forever, the killer and the killed written into history, memorialized or castigated.

To shun The Gun is to fear recklessness, to abhor chaos. Yet activists, oft called anarchistic, despise artists who don't overtly join them. Stanley Kunitz contends: "In a revolutionary period the activists are understandably disappointed in artists who do not overtly serve their movement. The Irish fighters for freedom despised [poet William Butler] Yeats for his failure to give them his unqualified support, not realizing that it was he who would immortalize their names and their cause…"

Bertolt Brecht said that a "conversation about trees is almost a crime because it involves keeping silent about so many misdeeds." The Black House in San Francisco flourished for a very short period (not as long as Felix Mitchell's drug empire) in 1966-67. I was there, and no one was talking trees. Eldridge Cleaver's book Soul on Ice was a bestseller, and playwright Marvin X had plays on at San Francisco State and in community theaters. They formed The Black House and opened it up for readings, political education classes, poetry and dance performances, jazz and lectures. In the Fillmore District, the Black House was a seemingly perfect black counterpart for the hippie and drug-oriented Haight-Asbury. But its split was not only political; in retrospect, its air had a chauvinist aura. Women were often ornamental, breeders not warriors, cooks and clericals, servers not speakers, as if there to divert the heavy thinkers from the heavy biz of the day – fighting the man.

Many cultural nationalists– LeRoi Jones [Amiri Baraka], Don Lee [Haki Madhubuti], Sonia Sanchez – were poets, and poets were the shining lights of the Black Arts Movement. Kunitz points out that the writer works alone, unlike other workers, and the poet is even more exceptional: "Among writers the poet is freer than his brothers the novelist and playwright, because his work, unlike theirs, is practically worthless as a commodity. He is less subject than they to the pressure to modify the quality of his work in order to produce an entertainment. Nothing he can do will make his labor profitable. He might as well yield to the beautiful temptation to strive towards the purity of an absolute art."

Thus when we see the Black Arts Movement and its relation to the BPP, the poets and dramatists stand in stark counterpoint. As student activists at San Francisco State, the Black Student Union fought to bring Jones, Lee and Sanchez onto campus. We formed the Black Arts and Culture Troupe and toured community centers throughout the Bay Area with poetry, dance, and agitprop plays. We enacted ideas we were hearing on soapboxes about black power, black consciousness and black beauty. We staged the conflagrations that were taking place in urban cities. We were empowering ourselves, our communities and getting academic credit. A natural progression was commu- nity activism. In 1967, my roommates and I joined the Black Panther Party which we found far more than a linguistic call to arms. It was a family, the place where you get together on holidays, tolerate the bigmouths, take care of each other, and keep it in the family, i.e. the secrets, the dirty laundry, the drunks, the incest, the beatings…. Robyn Spencer, who interviewed former Black Panther women in the 1990s for her doctoral research, commented at our final interview that she was frustrated by our overall lack of forthright- ness. I reminded her that there is no statute of limitations on murder, not that I knew of any such event.

However, the most important idea from that time was that we changed the language, the way black people thought and spoke, the way black people thought about how they were spoken about. A major assault on oppression is to assault it linguistically. Pre-Edward Said's Orientalism, two black males from the flatlands of Oakland, California, gave voice to the oppressed using English in a wholly new way. Jean-Paul Sartre said the oppressed gain the use of the oppressor's language. In one instant, Off the Pig tossed back all the awful, dehumanizing, negative ways African-Americans had been characterized for two centuries. Baboons, coons, animals. To come up with this one phrase to describe abominable behavior, not physicality, was genius.

In *Virgin Soul*, my coming-of-age novel about that time, I handle The Gun often. The narrative would have lost its essence if I hadn't. At one point, my protagonist Geniece shows her proper aunt the very first Black Panther Party newspaper. Her aunt recoils at the blood, guts and violence in Emory Douglas' artwork, with its copious use of the steely black metaphor. The Gun was an actual weapon carried and maintained by party members. It was Art. It was Metaphor. It was loaded with meaning and death.

The use of language and ritual had awed me in childhood where I loved communal gatherings, gospel fests, family and religious celebrations. I'd worked since high school as a journalist but became disgusted with the narrow scope of the field, its all-whiteness, sameness and predictability. Assigned to edit the BPP newspaper, I found myself embedded in the inner workings of the party, typing, retyping, printing words and phrases like off the pigs. Power to the people. All power to the people. Free Huey.

My hands shocked me as they lettered and typed these words and the manifestos they formed. The BPP was appropriating the oppressor's language and using it to shatter oppression. This new use of language by the BPP was as powerful as The Gun and even more so because it aroused feeling and changed the terms of discourse between friends, enemies, lovers, generations and cultures. Being an agent of change meant I aroused deep feeling, affected discourse, found the powerful voices that I had heard in childhood, in church, in soul music, in the pulpit – within my own voice. Thus empowered, I began writing poetry, essays, and eventually moved on to drama and fiction, my start as a writer.

Some would whitewash the civil rights movement and Dr. Martin Luther King Jr. into benign icons of a distant era, outsized statues or memories for annual celebration. Some would not see the movements for civil rights and black power nor the varied tactics of the NAACP, SCLC, SNCC, BPP, CORE, the Urban League, and the Nation of Islam as a spectrum of resistance against the racism that determined every facet of American life. The Black Panther Party for Self-Defense was the fist (The Gun, loaded, that is) of the kid (black people) who's been bullied (racism, oppression, legalized discrimination) long enough by the outsized bully on the block (US govt., US Constitution until 1865, opponents of Radical Reconstruction, Jim Crow, KKK, Bull Connor, etc.). "Power concedes nothing without a demand," Frederick Douglass said. To demand is not to ask or beseech. That time when the streets were packed with citizens, students, protestors, workers, mothers against the war, unionists was not an acquiescent moment in this country's history. The numerous deaths are memorialized and well-documented. Did the moment peter out? Vanish into thin air? Not quite. The principles spread into society.

From the virgin soil of turbulence came the second wave of feminism and gay rights movements. The disabled emerged from seclusion and institutions to lobby for public access and accommodations. Senior citizens became Gray Panthers. Maria Gillan [a friend and fellow poet] became Maria Mazziotti Gillan, reclaiming her Italian-American roots and triggering the ethnic white literary movement at once. Bilingualism and Ebonics became recognized as essential curricula. Caucus as an intransitive verb meant your group agenda had to be strengthened privately and exhaustively to have maximum impact. Self-help, self-empowerment and self-enhancement became ideals because an entire society had watched the 98-pound weakling (black people) go from chump to champ. Black music, musicians and dancers became ambassadors-at-large to American society and the world. Duke Ellington and Count Basie had been there, done that. But the airwaves and new media amplified the beat, the dances, the Soul Train lines, the frizzy hair, the handshakes, the lingo (bro), none of which needed The Gun or its bullet because the BPP had handled that task. Our current heated debate about the n-word is permissible because of the BPP and Black Arts and Culture movement. Ishmael Reed, in grand old man fashion, came out with *Writing is Fighting: Thirty-Seven Years of Boxing on Paper* in 1988. The feat of aging gives one that Yeatsian right to write the story.

A few years ago, I woke up surrounded by Guns. Guns. Guns. My boss at the state arts council hosted me at her South Jersey home during my artist-in-residency. We'd had a falling out after her son had been killed in a hunting accident and she'd had three months of disarray and grief. Without money to meet my basic expenses and no checks coming in, my capacity for sympathy plunged. Angry words ensued. Eventually we made up. She invited me to her beautiful, starkly contemporary home nestled in the woods. We drank wine and talked late into the night; I looked through photo albums as she recounted how her grown children had been hunting when one fired the bullet that ricocheted and hit her son. He died in surgery. I went to sleep in the spare bedroom, too tired to take a good look around me. I woke up an hour later and turned on the light. The room was decorated with guns – handguns, rifles and guns with bayonets mounted in wooden and glass cases. I was sleeping in an ordnance. I tried to fall asleep but couldn't dispel the images. In the moonlight I saw that the sheets on my bed had gun insignias all over them. For a moment, I thought I had gone crazy. Gun sheets? I had to do some serious calming down. The guns on the sheets and the walls were art, fashion and memorabilia.

I liked guns. I like mystery, intrigue, even devilment. My father was an avid reader of westerns, thrillers and detective novels. He had stacks of them next to his side of the bed. My mother had Bibles, loads of them, modern ones, illustrated ones, the King James Version. As far as I could tell he never read from her side, and she never read any of his books…complete opposites married for 50 years. There was no gun. My mother said we couldn't even have sharp knives because tempers were too short in our household.

I would like a society without The Gun. Too many short tempers in the world and this society. The BPP had a message that was received. As it deepened its focus in community service, the guns became purely metaphoric and the party split into factions for and against The Gun. Internecine rivalries sprung up. I had moved far away spatially and spiritually.

I don't want gun control. I want police who are unarmed, peace officers. We can't have that unless we do away with guns. Maybe we can have parks where people play with guns the way we play with dinosaurs. That sounds like a shooting range. But it wouldn't be for target practice. It would be for fun. It wouldn't be a rehearsal for cruelty.

When Trayvon Martin was killed by The Gun, my heart ached. Trayvon was at risk because he didn't know how to cower, a posture that my generation destroyed. He didn't turn tail and run – although he might just have been shot in the back; he didn't yessuh back stepping. He fought George Zimmerman, toe-to-toe, and Zimmerman fired The Gun, at point blank range, because that was his creative moment. His high art. His historical moment. George Zimmerman united with his opposite Trayvon Martin forever. And the performances continue, in Aurora, Illinois, in Newtown, Connecticut, in schools and theaters and public spaces throughout the country. I liked guns. I hate The Gun.

ain't supposed to die a natural death

below the fold of the nytimes
    wednesday august 23, 1989
        two deaths vie for attention
one begins
    Huey P. Newton, a co-founder of the Black Panther Party and a leader
    of a generation of blacks in the 1960's, was shot to death early today
    in the neighborhood where he began his organizing.
the other begins:
    Diana Vreeland, the legendary fashion editor and creator of spectac-
    ular fashion exhibitions at the Metropolitan Museum of Art in New
    York City, died of a heart attack yesterday at Lenox Hill Hospital. She
    was believed to be in her late 80's and had been in failing health for
    several years.
I sit at my desk drinking my morning coffee when my boss
who knows of my radical other life
spreads the nytimes before me:
"your boy went out in a blaze of glory"

Revolutionaries can't outlive the revolution. They risk becoming a despot.
Holding onto power. While the masses drive old Pontiacs in rural Cuba. They
turn into walking ghosts, living dinosaurs. Too big to be ignored, famous for
being famous. Spouting the rhetoric from a tape in their heads. Waiting, like
Che, for the Bolivian/CIA gawdzilla to execute him. Bobby Seale says in the
obit: "He and I should have lived to be old militant senior citizens." Not if
you're fighting gawdzilla. Huey becomes instead an icon.

Forever young.
Forever handsome
Forever 47 years old.

   gawdzilla is empire, whether you fight it or fashion it

Acknowledgements

Across The Margin
godzilla of innocence.
the biggest difference is not the money

Interlitq
Barney, the gawdzilla-training toy
d.j. raw product
I put everything she taught me in a snow globe
I try not to keep seeing jesus
when godzilla booted nixon out of the oval office

New Verse News
Dave Chappelle
godzilla as destiny (as "UP UP AND AWAY")
godzilla births female orangutans (as "APPROPRIATION")
godzilla 2022 (as "TIME'S UP")
lizzo fights godzilla (as "LIZZO")

The Weeklings
The Gun as Ultimate Performance Poem [nominated for a Pushcart Prize 2022]

About the Author

Judy Juanita's poetry collection, *Manhattan my ass, you're in Oakland*, won the American Book Award 2021 from the Before Columbus Foundation.

Her short story collection, *The High Price of Freeways*, won the Tartt Fiction Prize at the University of West Alabama [UWA], and was published by Livingston Press [UWA] in 2022.

Her semi-autobiographical novel, *Virgin Soul*, is about a young woman who joins the Black Panther Party in the 60s (Viking, 2013).

Her poem, "Bling," was nominated for a Pushcart Prize in 2012. Juanita's short stories and essays appear widely, and her poetry has appeared in *Obsidian II, KONCH, 13th Moon, Painted Bride Quarterly, Croton Review, The Passaic Review, Lips, New Verse News, Poetry Monthly, Drumrevue* and elsewhere.

Her essay, "The Gun as Performance Poem," and her short story, "The Black House," were nominated for the Pushcart Prize in 2014 and 2022, respectively.

Her 20+ plays have been produced in San Francisco, Oakland, Berkeley, L.A. and NYC, and are archived at the Jerome Lawrence and Robert E. Lee Theatre Research Institute at Ohio State University (OSU). "Theodicy," about two black men who accidentally fall into the river of death, was first runner-up in the Eileen Heckart Senior Drama Competition at OSU.

Her collection of essays, *DeFacto Feminism: Essays Straight Outta Oakland* [EquiDistance Press, 2016], examines the intersectionality of race, gender, politics, economics and spirituality as experienced by a black activist and self-described "feminist foot soldier." She is a contributing editor for The Weekling, an online journal, where many of the essays appeared. The collection was a distinguished finalist in OSU's 2016 Non/Fiction Collection Prize.

Her body of work, including books, plays, numerous drafts, recordings, articles and interviews, is archived at Duke University's John Hope Franklin Research Center for African and African American History and Culture alongside the archives of other 60s activists from SNCC and with the archives of fellow SFSU activist and her ex-husband/labor leader Clarence Carl Thomas Jr.

She teaches writing at University of California, Berkeley.

Gawdzilla is her second poetry collection.

Kirkus Reviews
Excerpts from kirkusreviews.com

"A Black Feminist Pioneer Looks Back" by Rhett Morgan.

In De Facto Feminism, *you refer to yourself as an "observational ironist." How does this sum up your style as a writer?*

I'm a "Kibbles and Bits" writer. I'm always making notes, scribbling on Post-its and envelopes. And I get my sense of irony from my dad, who was a very sarcastic person....I eventually learned that sarcasm is a mark of high intelligence. So, I flatter myself to say that I observe closely and I see the absurdity in human life. But, it's really just a fancy term to say that I check things out.

How have your experiences self-publishing differed from working with a major publisher?

One of the main differences was that there is a small window of time with traditional publishers. It helps to get their stamp of approval, but exposure and publicity with them was only from the day [*Virgin Soul*] came out to about three months later. It was just the opposite with *De Facto Feminism*, which took off slowly but is still getting responses. To me, the benefit of self-publishing is keeping your work alive. Once you've self-published, it's there forever unless you take it down.

Do you think that self-publishing can open doors for more diverse voices?

Yes, because you can get to your own audiences, especially if you are a person of color or a person who has a specialized audience. One of my friends told me, "Do Oakland. Do you." So, that's what I did, and colleges here have taken up my books. I also learned an important lesson on my book tour. I saw very successful authors who had their book from traditional publishers and [others with] their books through indie presses. And they were all selling. It wasn't as though the buyers made some huge distinction. They were buying books just because they were by these authors.

You joined the Black Panthers when you were a student. What do you want to see today's young African Americans do to combat racism and fight for equality?

I want my students to have historical awareness. I want them to be aware of the factors involved in situating them where they are today. The break-throughs that came from the Black Power and civil rights movements, those were so historic and fulfilled one part of the promise of the American independence. They need to understand those factors so they can under-stand why a Beyoncé and a Jay-Z can exist and have incredible power, why a Barack Obama can come along seven generations after the Emancipation Proclamation.

You've written about "avoiding African American chick lit." What do you wish you saw more of on bookshelves from African American women?

It's a critique but not a slam against those books. Anything that gets people reading is fine with me. My hope is that we penetrate all the genres. That's it. Like Barbara Neely, a mystery writer who recently passed away and wrote about a black maid that solved murders. Other people are able to write anything. Why shouldn't we? Sometimes they want to file us just under "Black Authors." We should be all over the place....James Joyce, you know, he was not just an "Irish Writer."

Praise for Manhattan my ass, you're in Oakland

"What a distinctive, powerful, undaunted, sane, straight-shooting, de facto feminist voice! I fucking love hearing the voice on these pages."

— *Gail Wronsky*, Poems for Infidels, Dying for Beauty

"Feisty, often humorous, and philosophical. It's also passionate and filled with local spirit...But this book is not just for Oaklanders. The poems contain wisdom and entertainment for people in Manhattan, Oakland, and every-where in between."

— *Lucille Lang Day*, Married at Fourteen: A True Story, Fire and Rain: Ecopoetry of California

"A renowned novelist, poet, and playwright, [Juanita] showcases her deft use of numerous styles of poetry and modified prose in her new book. Many of the pieces are set against the backdrop of rough-and-tumble Oakland while invoking the legacies and lessons of black poets like Dudley Randall and Langston Hughes. Permeated with themes of sexual and racial inequality, this collection of 50-plus pieces fittingly begins with a credo against toxic masculinity, conjuring the Greek figure of Lysistrata. Similarly sexually charged imagery is often featured throughout the volume. These subtle and not-so-subtle erotic performances juxtapose the viciously practical with the beautiful. A classically structured sonnet dissects how "brothers get ferocious when they fuck" while another poem includes the lines "softly pull nipples to hard ripple cord come / after checking for lumps." This isn't the only way the work subverts readers' expectations; the collection often injects bodily disgust or mental discomfort into the pieces to catch the audience off guard. A return home to the staleness of a father-run household is punctuated by a scream-ing enema. A humorous prose piece about the use of the n-word is made all the more unsettling by the fact that it's predicated on the death of a Latino man who should not have been uttering the slur in the first place. Keeping readers on edge like this is an effective tactic to drive home the importance of the subjects addressed. One poem considers men needing women to be their props a systemic issue. In another piece, the ethereal imagery of downtrodden egg- and worm-eaters' rising up to reach a dispassionate white angel remains striking in its symbolism....Modern and historical hallmarks of social justice are present throughout, from Donald Trump's rise and Harvey Weinstein's crimes to the acquittal of O.J. Simpson, Sarah Palin's "babymommadrama," and the Gulf War....Unsettling, important, and unforgettable poetry."

— *Kirkus Reviews*

"Oakland can't get no respect. The towns surrounding it don't want to be associated with it. Judy Juanita even points to sections of Oakland that don't wish to be associated with it. Blacks are profiled in the Rockridge section of Oakland, which Juanita calls 'pretend Berkeley.' Berkeley is the Whitest city in Alameda County regardless of its radical reputation. A city where one might be profiled even at cultural institutions. Both Juanita and I were profiled at the Berkeley Repertory Theater. In her book *Manhattan my ass, you're in Oakland*, Juanita gives the history of Oakland before the expulsion of Blacks from the city by the banks, the police and Jerry Brown. With the invasion of the city by Millennials, will Oakland become Berkeley? Not If Judy Juanita has anything to do about it. Juanita stands up for a city that is more than a place where surrounding cities dump their trash."

— *Ishmael Reed*

Publishers Weekly starred review of *De Facto Feminism: Essays Straight Outta Oakland*

The essays in this collection from poet and novelist Juanita *(Virgin Soul)* provide a dynamic and illuminating take on a distinct subset of feminism nurtured by Oakland, Calif.'s community, as well as the story of Juanita's coming of age as an artist. She provides vivid glimpses into her childhood in the 1950s in East Oakland and describes becoming aware of the "high status of light skin and non kinky hair," along with her experiences in the Black Panther Party while attending S.F. State University in the 1960s and how it all came to inform her identity as a black woman activist. Juanita presents a slew of cultural factors including TV and the Beatles as contributing to the black revolution, the black arts movement, and the rise of black women's feminism as a distinctive movement. She uses the term "de facto feminist" to describe herself, and black women in general: "De facto feminism is like de facto segregation, which remains the way our nation is organized. De facto segregation is the practical reality of separation of members of different races, not by law... but in practice by various social and economic factors." Personal reminiscences ("We were the first family on the block to visit Disneyland") mixed with pop culture details ("At a Beatles concert in Plymouth, Great Britain, in November 1963, police used high-pressure hoses on screaming fans, a show of authority that matched the hosing of demonstrators in Birmingham six months earlier") create a rhythmic and unforgettable portrait of an artist and activist coming of age. *(BookLife)*

A Few Things Judy Juanita's De Facto Feminism Got Me Thinking About

Chris Stroffolino's book review [excerpted] of De Facto Feminism: Essays Straight Outta Oakland, **Konch**, *Ishmael Reed's online magazine, December 2016*

I always felt that one of the reasons the Occupy Wall Street 99% movement (of 2011/12) was doomed to failure, aside from hostile external forces like the police, the corporate media, and the ostensibly non-political real estate market, was because there was a wall of misunderstanding between those who set up the occupy camps (where everyone gets 5 minutes to speak at a microphone), and those fighting more through the formal mediation of art, writing, or recorded music. Ex-Black Panther, and "lone wolf," Judy Juanita's new *De Facto Feminism: Essays Straight Outta Oakland* (2016) sheds many insights into these dynamics in ways that can be useful for any future artists and activists who wish to work together to form a movement that may topple the patriarchal, plutocratic, racist imperialism that dominates American reality in an era of global capitalism. She understands the psychology in which "activists, oft called anarchistic, despise artists who don't overtly join them." Some feel it's an unequal trade, that somehow the artists aren't giving back what they're receiving. In any event, I've heard many activists scold the very people they're trying to recruit, or seduce, "you're acting too much like an individualist, a *bourgeois* individualist."

In *De Facto Feminism*, Judy Juanita celebrates the *working class* black individualist...by showing the (oft-unheralded) ways they help build community, not through theoretical imperative, but simply in order to survive. The women Juanita celebrates transcend the false "binary thinking dilemmas" (between artist and activist, and between individualist and collectivist) to engage in an artistic activism, and an altruism that need not be self-abnegating that occupies a fertile, proliferative, place where selfishness and altruism, individualism and community activism can unite. For sometimes the reason why one doesn't fit in to one social scene is the same reason you can get along with more people from *other* social scenes.

For Juanita, this has been a life-long struggle, "an act of self-creation spanning 4 decades," and *De Facto Feminism* is a record of her findings that can be useful for current and future generations of artists and activists in their struggles.

During her time with the Black Panthers, which in hindsight she calls her phase of "naively determined black womanhood," Juanita had been an idealistic anti-individualist collectivist (In "Black Womanhood," an essay Juanita wrote at the age of 20 for the *Black Panther Newspaper,* she writes that the struggle requires "her strength, not her will, her leadership, her domination, but her strength"). But, it must not be forgotten that Juanita, even as a young woman, was not just a Black Panther, but also part of the Black Arts Movement (BAM which may not be as well known to the general reader).

> "As student activists at SF State, the Black Student Union fought to bring Jones (Baraka), Lee (Mudhubuti) and Sanchez onto Campus. We formed the Black Arts and Culture Troupe and toured community centers throughout the Bay Area with poetry, dance and agit-prop plays. We enacted ideas we were hearing on soap-boxes about black power, black consciousness, and black beauty. We staged mock conflagrations like ones that were taking place in urban cities. We were empowering ourselves, our communities and getting academic credit. A natural progression was community activism."

When she joined the Black Panthers, she was drawn to the alliance between artists and activists, but witnessed, during an era of "shattering community," a growing split between the two groups: "to look at the BAM and its relation to the BPP renders a vision of the poets and the dramatists standing in counterpoint." Ultimately, however,

> "the activists upstaged the artist/intellectuals. I had immense sympathy for the second group, but pitied them (pitied their women more. How much subservience would soothe a wounded ego?)"

Despite the chauvinism she found in the BAM more than in the BPP, and the factionalism and her torn allegiances, Juanita appreciated what the BPP and Black Arts Movement had in common, and celebrates this legacy:

> "The BPP was appropriating the oppressors' language, and using it to shatter oppression. That new use of language, in the BPP and the BAM, was as powerful as any gun, and even more powerful because it aroused feeling and changed the terms of discourse between friends, enemies, lovers, generations and cultures. Being an agent of change meant I aroused deep feelings, affected discourse, found the powerful voices that I had heard in childhood, in church, in soul music, in the pulpit — in my own voice."

Juanita's allegiance was both to art and to activism, and she didn't want to be forced to choose, and as we see her mind go back and forth between the BPP and the BAM, weighing the advantages of each and trying to develop a new synthesis, we see her ability to step back from the heated conflicts and tense divisiveness between the artists and activists to see the productive symbiosis:

> "Black music, musicians and dancers became ambassadors at
> large to the world. But the airwaves and new media amplified
> the beat, the dances, the Soul Train lines, the frizzy hair, the
> handshakes, the lingo (bro), now of which needed the Gun or its
> bullet because the BPP handled that task,"

Part of the reason the BPP was able to handle the task is because of what
women like Judy Juanita (aka Judy Hart) provided.

As we celebrate the 50th anniversary of both the BAM and the BPP, the role
of women in the Black Panther party (which was numerically mostly women)
is still not emphasized enough in biopics like the recent PBS *Vanguard of
The Revolution,* (2016), yet even in *Seize The Time* (1970), Bobby Seale wrote
of the first women in the Black Panther's power to educate and recruit new
members to the party. Juanita, ex-editor-in-chief of the *Black Panther* newspaper, gives her own account of the importance of these young women as
bringing together rival factions to create and sustain a larger, more rooted,
movement. Certainly, Juanita and the other women were no passive recipients
of edicts from Bobby, Huey, and Eldridge:

> "Our gang of five affected policy and high-level decisions by
> virtue of our intense participation, outspokenness....we also
> formed liaisons and romantic relationships with brothers in the
> party. From the upper echelon to the lumpen proletariat, we
> lived, slept, ate and cooked with the BPP.... We were the initial
> link between the campus and the party. Three of us married
> 'brothers in the struggle' who also happened to be educated
> brothers. This is significant because our connections and intimacy
> (which some labeled promiscuity) connected brothers from the
> party with brothers from SF State. The BSU brothers like to talk
> about supplying the BPP with guns and money, but this bridge
> called my back supplied the people's army with equal and great-
> er provision."

This final point provides a great example of what the mature Juanita refers
to as "De Facto Feminism." In her title essay, she offers her own definition
of "de facto feminism" by contrasting it with the 20th century feminism she
experienced:

20th Century feminism is "defensive, lean-in elite, scarce, historical, white-ish, precious, theoretical, lawful, contempt for men but
not their $$$." De Facto feminism is "offensive, classless, prolif-
erative, a historical, black and then some, inside/outside the law,
do you with/without men.

This contrast does not get tangled up in the academic debates between the
"difference" and "sameness" feminists, but is a celebration of the practical
de facto feminists who "stand between peace and war every day in…the Gaza
Strips of the US" in the absence of being able to change the laws. Although
she claims de facto feminism is "classless," it's clear that it is working class as
Juanita never loses sight of the economic dimensions to patriarchal sexism,
especially when coupled with "the stigma that black people carry as pigment"
that

"forces them to be what others would term illegal, immoral but
not impractical. A whole class of workers constitutes women
who braid hair, part of the underground economy in the black
community. Overwhelmingly black and youthful, they work
from home, a cadre of postmodern kitchen beauticians who make
a way out of no way, to raise children, make money, be stylish
and create community."

All of the women Juanita celebrates in this essay, she boldly claims, "are far
more feminist than the broadcast/weathercasters who've memorized feminist
principles and theory from prep school through Ivy League. Juanita also
nods to the women who founded BlackLivesMatters when she writes, "a
new wave of feminists instead might envision women of color setting policy
and leading, being arbiters instead of being left behind," and I think of the
LaughingWhileBlack women scolded by a white woman on the Napa Valley
Wine Train (2015), and their unheralded contributions to the legal corporate
economy when Juanita celebrates the book clubs that gave "mainstream
publishing a shot in the arm."

Reminding us that "in protest movements, as in wars, the people on the
bottom don't write history," Juanita uses her literate skills throughout *De Facto
Feminism* to speak of, to, and for, those de facto closer to "the bottom," and
asks

"will it take 200 years for respect to come to those de facto
feminists sitting on the bottom, squeezed into pink collar ghettos
and brown security guard uniforms lined up at the minimum
wage margins of this world?"

Although Juanita expresses a justifiable disgust with "the white-ish, lean-in elite" characteristics that is the legacy of dominant 20th century (second-wave) feminism, her book does contain one instance that celebrates the de facto (rather than de jure) feminism of the white women. During her adolescence in 1964, during the period when Sly Stone wrote "The Swim," and helped create a dance craze working closely with white topless dancer Carol Doda, Juanita writes of the powerful convergence that The Birth Control Bill and Beatles created for whites. As a teenage Juanita watches young white women starting to dance more with black women (even as their parents are leaving the neighborhood), she notices:

> "All the prepubescent and adolescent white girls having orgasmic and orgiastic responses released a long suppressed sexuality from its Victorian, Southern, and Puritan constraints. As these women let it rip in that prolonged moment of free public expression, they freed up black women from whoredom, from bearing the brunt and hard edge of the white men's sexuality. We were no longer the only culturally-sanctioned object of naughty or forbidden sex, of plantation promiscuity."

This is one instance where young white women — by liberating themselves — were able to do more to liberate black women than any of their paternalistic Moynihan-Report inflected proclamations could....or would. Juanita's perspective on this time when de-segregation seemed promising through music and dance should be must reading for any historian of the swinging sixties sick of the Male Baby Boomer Rock Critic establishment's version (Greil Marcus, et al) and, shows, the ways in which the more ostensibly "apolitical" music of the early 60s (the groundswell from the segregated R&B stations) had more power than 70s "profound" light rock whose rise paralleled the rise of white-ish feminism.

And, finally, she offers a powerful argument for why whites should care, and not just for "altruistic" (paternalistic) reasons, but yes, for selfish reasons.

> "Black people often serve as an early warning system for the American populace...for better and worse, the hardcore issues blacks face — guns, crime, poverty, failing schools — define the newest America."

As the standard of living for most whites in America has been noticeably decreasing since the great crash of 2008 (although not as much as it is for blacks), Juanita reminds me a little of those women at the Occupy Rally with the "Blacks have always been the 99%" sign.

I'm a woman. POW! Black. BAM! Outspoken. STOMP! Don't fit
in. OUCH! The lesson? Sometimes when one takes a stand one
becomes a lone wolf, a neighborhood of one, a community of one
to declare sovereignty for art, sexuality, spirituality, and say-so,
an individual."

De Facto Feminism, however, includes a much more varied range of writing
than my essayistic explorations of two of its more publically-inflected threads
may suggest to one who hasn't read it. Even if you have no interest in the
Panthers, or community activism, or in feminism, per se, there are many
personally-inflected essays that focus on her life as a writer. It is not merely
a series of essayistic arguments, but maintains "the feel of memoir" as these
essays are a loosely constructed chronology/autobiographical journey.
Eschewing the fictional mask of the "unreliable narrator" Geniece in her
semi-autobiographical *Virgin Soul*, the political and the personal come even
closer in *De Facto Feminism*, as Juanita casts a retrospective glance from which
to build a present and future, without debilitating nostalgia.

Because Juanita published *Virgin Soul* (2013), in her late 60s, what people
used to call one's retirement years (when one could get away doing that),
some may see her as a late bloomer. Yet, what Juanita was doing these years,
was not merely honing her craft, but also exploring different social dynamics
in which art circulates (as she explores the social interactions in the theatre
world, the stand-up comedy world, and even the poetry world), and also
digesting (if not exactly recoiling from) the extremely intense baptism by fire
she experienced at age 20 in the Black Panthers as an agent of change. The
years in between are hardly lost years. Juanita is able to make art out of her
stint as a maid in "Cleaning Other People's Houses," in addition to increas-
ing her empathy for the working class women she champions. In a sense, the
essay on Carolyn Rogers may be the most personal, as obviously Juanita can
relate to a woman celebrated by the BAM, but later forgotten as she eschewed
the militant posture which made it easier to get published during this time.

In these essays, Juanita emerges as a working class artist/intellectual (which
our dominant culture tries to tell us is an oxymoron), one who is highly
skeptical of the ready-made solutions, and the ridiculous gerrymandered
specialized genres. She challenges the social nexus that too often determines
the circulation of literary texts in our society, and yet emerges triumphant.
As she speaks of the way she learned to become a novelist, by jumping from
many social scenes and roles as artist/intellectual, I see a writer relentlessly
measuring the inner world by the outer world, and vice versa.

CPSIA information can be obtained
at www.ICGtesting.com
Printed in the USA
BVHW061317050123
655630BV00005B/155

9 781732 609808